TITLE I MATERIALS

Georgetown Elementary School
Indian Prairie School District
Aurora, Illinois

Joe-Joe the Wizard Brews Up
Solids, Liquids, and Gases

by Eric Braun

illustrated by Robin Boyden

PICTURE WINDOW BOOKS
a capstone imprint

Thanks to our advisers for their expertise, research, and advice:
Dr. Paul Ohmann, Associate Professor of Physics, University of St. Thomas
Terry Flaherty, PhD, Professor of English, Minnesota State Universty, Mankato

Editor: **Gillia Olson**
Designer: **Lori Bye**
Art Director: **Nathan Gassman**
Production Specialist: **Danielle Ceminsky**
The illustrations in this book were created digitally.

Picture Window Books
1710 Roe Crest Drive
North Mankato, MN 56003
www.capstonepub.com

 All books published by Picture Window Books
are manufactured with paper containing at least
10 percent post-consumer waste.

Library of Congress Cataloging-in-Publication Data
Braun, Eric, 1971–
 Joe-Joe the wizard brews up solids, liquids, and gases / written by
Eric Braun ; illustrated by Robin Boyden.
    p. cm. — (In the science lab)
 Includes bibliographical references and index.
 ISBN 978-1-4048-7147-2 (library binding) — ISBN 978-1-4048-7238-7 (paperback)
 1. Matter—Properties—Juvenile literature. 2. Change of state
(Physics)—Experiments—Juvenile literature. 3. Solids—Juvenile
literature. 4. Liquids—Juvenile literature. 5. Gases—Juvenile
literature. I. Boyden, Robin, 1983– ill. II. Title.
 QC173.36.B73 2012
 530.4—dc23   2011029680

Printed in the United States of America in North Mankato, Minnesota.
       102011   006405CGS12

Joe-Joe is a student at Ms. Tickle's Academy of Magic. His favorite class is "Spells for Bad Smells." Sometimes he doesn't do his homework, though, and he gets in trouble. Once, he made up a spell that doubled his name. He didn't learn how to change it back, and now he's Joe-Joe.

Joe-Joe's least favorite class is Regular Old Science. Today in that class they were studying something called states of matter. Boring! So Joe-Joe brewed a potion to turn his Regular Old Science homework into chocolate bars.

3

But he made a mistake, and the homework turned into chocolate syrup instead. "What happened here, Joe-Joe?" asked his teacher, Ms. Tickle. "What were you trying to do?"

"Me? Uh, nothing," said Joe-Joe.

"ISN'T THIS YOUR HOMEWORK?" said Ms. Tickle.

"YOU TURNED YOUR HOMEWORK INTO CHOCOLATE SYRUP?"

4

Joe-Joe looked at the floor. "I was trying to turn it into chocolate bars," he said.

Ms. Tickle smiled. "It's a good thing we're studying states of matter," she said. "You have a lot to learn."

"Matter is boring," Joe-Joe said. Then he added, "By the way, what is matter?"

"Matter is what everything in the universe is made of," said Ms. Tickle. "From dirt to dump trucks. From animals to apple juice. Even air is made of matter."

"EVEN AIR?" asked Joe-Joe. "SO WHAT MAKES MATTER MATTER?"

"Anything that has mass, or weight, is matter," answered Ms. Tickle. "You don't think of air as weighing anything, but it does. It just weighs very little compared to other things, like chocolate syrup."

APPLE JUICE

6

"OK. But what about these 'states'?" asked Joe-Joe.

"Right," said Ms. Tickle. "Matter comes in three states—solid, liquid, and gas. A chocolate bar would be a solid. Chocolate syrup is a liquid. Get it?"

Joe-Joe bit his lip, thinking. "Not really."

7

Ms. Tickle said, "LIQUIDS, LIKE WATER, MILK, AND CHOCOLATE SYRUP, FLOW."

"LIKE GO WITH THE FLOW?" asked Joe-Joe.

"Sort of. To flow means to slide around and change shape. A liquid takes the same shape as its container."

★ DRAGON TEARS ★

Finest Newt Juice

"OKAY, I GET IT," said Joe-Joe.

"THERE SURE IS A LOT OF THIS LIQUID."

"Even though liquids do not have a definite shape, they do have a definite volume," said Ms. Tickle.

"Yes, I can hear it dripping," said Joe-Joe.

"Not volume as in how loud it is," said Ms. Tickle. "Volume means how much space it takes up. Chocolate syrup takes up as much space in a bottle as it does on the floor. It would look different in the bottle, but it would have the

"**WHAT IF I DRANK IT ALL?**" asked Joe-Joe.

"It would take up the same space," said Ms. Tickle. "But it would be space inside you."

"**WELL, EATING HOMEWORK WOULD BE MORE FUN THAN DOING IT,**" said Joe-Joe.

Chocolate Spells 101.
Please ask the teacher for permission before trying out these spells.

CHOC MILK

CHOC SYRUP

"Wow, this liquid is getting everywhere," Joe-Joe said. "Can you change it?"

"SHALL I ABRACA-ZAP IT INTO A SOLID?" Ms. Tickle asked.

"Chocolate bars? Oh, yes please," said Joe-Joe.

12

Ms. Tickle waved her wand at the liquid and said, "ABRACA-ZAP!"
The liquid began to gather into a solid shape—the
shape of one big chocolate bar.

"Yum," said Joe-Joe. He reached for the chocolate.

"Hold on," said Ms. Tickle.

"Aw!" said Joe-Joe. That chocolate looked good.

"How is the solid different from the liquid?" asked Ms. Tickle.

"It keeps its shape," Joe-Joe said.

"Right. Do you think you could change that shape?"

Joe-Joe's mouth was watering.

"YOU COULD BREAK IT UP AND EAT IT."

"Right again, Joe-Joe. A solid holds a certain shape. Its shape can be changed, but it takes some force. A chocolate bar is easy to break—or eat. To change the shape of a rock, though, you'd need a lot more force."

"What about volume?" asked Joe-Joe. "If you change the shape of a solid, does it keep the same volume, like a liquid does?"

"Yes," said Ms. Tickle. "There is only one state of matter that changes volume. That's gas."

Ms. Tickle waved her wand over the chocolate bar and said,

"ABRACA-DIZZLE!"

The chocolate bar began to dissolve and float into the air.
"There," said Ms. Tickle. "Now we have chocolate gas."

"I've never heard of chocolate gas before," said Joe-Joe.

16

"Me neither," said Ms. Tickle. "But look how it expands. That means it grows. It is changing shape and volume. Only a gas does that. It expands and constantly changes shape."

"What are some other gases?" asked Joe-Joe.

"Oxygen is a gas," said Ms. Tickle. "The air we breathe is a mixture of gases, including oxygen."

"Ms. Tickle, lots of people can't do magic. How do they change matter from one state to another?" asked Joe-Joe.

"Good question," said Ms. Tickle. "You can change the state of matter by changing its temperature. Heat a solid to a high enough temperature, and it will turn into a liquid. If you keep raising the temperature, the liquid turns into a gas. The opposite happens when you lower the temperature."

"Oh, like water," Joe-Joe said.

"Water is a liquid. But if you make water super cold, it turns to ice, which is a solid. And if you boil it, it turns to steam. Is steam a gas?"

Ms. Tickle nodded.

"But wait," Joe-Joe said.
"Anything can change states?"

"Sure," said Ms. Tickle. "Most substances are in their natural state at room temperature. Water is liquid. Bricks are solid. The temperature to change a substance from one state to another depends on the substance."

Joe-Joe said, "I remember that ice turns to liquid at 32 degrees Fahrenheit (0 degrees Celsius). But pumpkins turn to liquid at ... well, at a higher temperature."

"You're a fast learner, Joe-Joe," said Ms. Tickle. "And don't worry. I can make another copy of your homework."

"Oh, great," said Joe-Joe sadly.

"And I can do something else for you too," said Ms. Tickle. She waved her wand again, and said, "Abraca-doodle!" A small black cloud went poof! above Joe-Joe's head.

"What happened?" he said.

"I changed your name. Now you're just Joe again."

"Thanks!" said Joe. And then he started on his solid new homework.

22

GLOSSARY

expand—to grow and spread out

gas—a substance that spreads to fill any space that holds it

liquid—a wet substance that flows and takes the shape of its container

mass—the amount of matter in an object or substance

matter—anything that has weight and takes up space

solid—a substance that holds its shape

volume—the amount of space something takes up

TO LEARN MORE

More Books to Read

Biskup, Agnieska. *The Solid Truth about States of Matter with Max Axiom, Super Scientist.* Graphic Science. Mankato, Minn.: Capstone Press, 2009.

Brent, Lynnette. *States of Matter.* Why Chemistry Matters. Crabtree Publishing Company, 2009.

Cook, Trevor. *Experiments with States of Matter.* Science Lab. New York: PowerKids Press, 2009.

Monroe, Tilda. *What Do You Know about States of Matter?* 20 Questions: Physical Science. New York: PowerKids Press, 2011.

Internet Sites

FactHound offers a safe, fun way to find Internet sites related to this book. All of the sites on FactHound have been researched by our staff.

Here's all you do:

Visit *www.facthound.com*

Type in this code: 9781404871472

Super-cool stuff! Check out projects, games and lots more at www.capstonekids.com

Index

Look For All the Books in the Series:

Captain Kidd's Crew Experiments with

Sinking and Floating

DO-4U the Robot Experiences

Forces and Motion

Gertrude and Reginald the Monsters Talk about

Living and Nonliving

Joe-Joe the Wizard Brews Up

Solids, Liquids, and Gases